D

the RICH
SWITCH

The *Simple* 3-Step System To
TURN ON INSTANT WEALTH
Using the Law of Attraction

For more information on this series, please visit us on the web at
RichSwitch.com.

ISBN 978-1-60842-002-5

KRE, LLC
PO Box 121135
Nashville, TN 37212-1135

Contents

Preface

I had just turned 16 when a friend came over to visit wearing a very nice, full-length cashmere coat. It was the kind of coat a successful businessman would wear, but we were both in high school and the only money we had was from working part-time scooping ice cream at a Baskin-Robbins store, so I knew he must have gotten it as a gift.

"My grandfather gave it to me," he said. "But he made me read a book first."

That book was *As a Man Thinketh* by James Allen.

"It's a good book," my friend said.

A few days later, when I saw him again, he said to me, "I told my grandfather you liked my coat. He said he has a similar one for you, if you'll read the book, like I did."

I wanted that coat, so I took him up on the offer. Imagine my surprise when the book was smaller than a deck of cards and only a few pages! A pretty good deal, I thought…

That was my first exposure to what has become known as the Law of Attraction. And my side of "the deal" has been much better than a nice coat to wear.

It's been several years since this happened, but the concept Earl Nightingale described as "The Strangest Secret" has stuck with me in all aspects of my life, from personal to business. In short, "We become what we think about."

I've written several books on the subject of Law of Attraction, especially when it comes to wealth building. This book, *The Rich Switch*, is my version of the book that was handed to me as a teenager. It's short and direct, without any filler.

The Rich Switch takes the most powerful concepts behind the Law of Attraction and breaks them down into an easy-to-implement, 3-step formula. When put together, these three steps yield powerful results.

The formula within this book has worked for millions of people. It will work for you.

Like my friend's grandfather, I hope you'll find this information worthy enough to share with others in your life. It is truly life-changing and a powerful way to affect the world in a positive way.

Thank you!

David Hooper
Nashville, TN

Getting Started

How to Get What You Want—Right Now

Are you wondering why you haven't already had more success in your life? If so, you're not alone. In fact, if you want more success in your life, especially in the areas of career, money, relationships, and health, you *should* be wondering.

Deep within us is an ability for massive success so powerful that nothing can stop it. This innate ability is what I refer to as "The Rich Switch." If you're not aware such power exists, it's because you haven't yet learned how to turn it on.

"The Rich Switch" isn't just about money, although that is what a great portion of this book focuses on, since money is so easy to attain. "The Rich Switch" is about wealth in all its forms. You can use it to improve your relationships, health, or whatever else you'd like.

So how do you activate it?

If you compare yourself to other people, it's easy to wonder why they may be more successful than you. It's no secret that different people achieve a widely varying amount of success in their lives. You have probably made these observations at some point, and wondered why this is true. Why does success among people vary so widely? And why does this success not always correspond to where these people are living, who they are, or what their backgrounds have been?

Have you ever seen a "rich" person lose everything, only to have it all back (and then some) within months?

Did you know about 80% of lottery winners, even those who win multi-million dollar jackpots, are broke within five years of winning? In fact, they actually have less money after five years than they did the day before they won.

How does this happen?

The answer in both cases… The Rich Switch.

Here's the good news…

It is possible to activate The Rich Switch and learn the key methods of how to manifest all you desire and apply these elements to all aspects of your life. Once you begin to believe it is possible to create the life you want based on your thoughts, you'll start seeing results right away.

I used to wonder why there were so many differences in the levels of success and happiness of people around the world. As a result, I made it one of my goals to find out what makes certain people better at attracting the lives of their dreams. I hoped, once I had the answer to that question, I could change my life and pass along what I had learned so you could change yours as well.

Changing *your* life is the purpose of this book and exactly what it will help you to do.

Here's more good news for you which will make the process easy!

I've found a short series of instructions on how to manifest with ease. They are very simple and easy to follow. You can use these instructions at anytime in your own life to manifest money, success, and happiness. Trust me, these instructions work if you give them a try. You will find that the results will appear to be magic, although it really isn't magic at all.

These instructions have been producing amazing results for people just like you for centuries. There is no restriction as to how often or how much you can use them.

Don't worry if your friends or family tell you the steps you are about to learn can't possibly work. Just remember, there is always someone who will be telling you something is impossible.

The majority of human beings are great at focusing on what can't be done...or what they think can't be done. Yet how many things which were "impossible" at one time are now being done on a daily basis? Nothing is impossible. We use that word not for things that can't be done, but for things that haven't been done...*yet*.

Henry Ford said it best when he said, "Whether you believe you can do a thing or not, you are right."

What you will achieve in life is based on your expectations. You have all the power you need already within you to manifest your dreams, hopes, and desires and watch them become reality.

When you follow the short set of instructions presented in this book, you will start seeing your dreams come true. You will find that you are getting great results both quickly and easily.

The Rich Switch is already within you; it simply needs to be activated in order to work properly. Like a light switch, this can be done instantly, if you know how. By the time you finish this book, you'll know exactly how, since I've broken this process down into simple steps that are easy to follow and understand.

The Power of Words…

Before we get started on Step One, it's important that you understand the great power of words. This is especially true for words written on paper.

If you were to take a piece of paper and write a letter to your mother, you would get a totally different result with the words "I love you" than you would with the words "I hate you."

Even reading these different examples probably gave you a different emotional reaction. Yet, the message is done with the same ink and on the same paper. Just one word makes all the difference…

This is the power of words.

Unlike spoken words, words on paper are a physical manifestation of thought. In other words, you have a thought in your head and are translating that to something you can hold, rather than something intangible. Speaking your truth, via words, is extremely important and powerful, but words translated into something physical give them special power.

All of us have had a verbal argument at one time or another. During arguments, words are often spoken without thought. Although this can be hurtful, it's nothing like the hurt of "Poison Pen" letters, which require more effort to create and can be viewed again and again by the recipient, wounding again each time.

Anybody who has received a "Dear John" letter can relate to this!

The power of the written word is massive. Fortunately, this power works both ways, and can be used for something positive. For this reason, writing your desires on paper is the first step in activating the Rich Switch.

STEP ONE:
Write It to Ignite It

The first step to activate the Rich Switch within you is to keep a written journal of the things you want. Keep this list in a special place and review it several times per day.

Read the instructions below. Commit them to memory. You may think writing a list of your desires sounds simple and may not make a difference. However, remember that your words have power and making a physical manifestation of those words, in the form of a list, has even greater power.

Focusing your power is what makes the Rich Switch work, so follow each step for best results.

1. Write a list of all the things you want in your life. While you are writing and thinking about your list, don't censor yourself. Don't tell yourself that any of your goals are too big or impossible to attain. Instead, write what your heart and soul truly desire.

2. When you have your list ready, review it *at least* three times each day. At the very minimum, review your list when you get up in the morning, around lunchtime, and again before you go to bed.

3. In addition to reviewing your list, at other times of the day keep your focus on your goals and how it would *feel* to have already accomplished them.

4. Do not discuss your ideas or what you want with anyone. Keep it all inside your mind. Remember, the source within you has a power that will manifest these desires. Don't worry about forcing any kind of schedule for manifesting your results. They will come to you at the quickest and best time possible. Setting a schedule would limit this.

NOTE: The one exception to the rule about not discussing your ideas or goals with others is when you are talking about things within an organized "mastermind" group. I'll give you details about mastermind groups and how to form one for yourself later in the book.

At a certain point, your objective mind will deliver to you a strategy for accomplishing your goals. It is for this reason that, as you make your list, you should *not* focus on "how" you will get the things on it. Thinking about the "how" too early in the process will limit the list of what you really want to what you consciously think you can achieve.

Your "thinking mind" will be your biggest obstacle to activating the Rich Switch and letting it work for you. The process is not logical, so don't "think" about it. Just make the list. The information you need about *how* things will happen will come to you later in the process and it will be automatic, so no "thinking" is required.

Don't worry if the items on your list keep changing. It is very common for things to change and adapt as you add new wants and desires. As people change, plans change.

Changing and adapting what you want is a very normal and natural phenomenon. If you feel what you want is changing, just embrace this feeling and go with it. You are doing everything perfectly. If you start to hear a little voice in the back of your head tell you that you will never achieve the goals on your list and that they are impossible, simply ignore that voice. The best way to do this is to fill your mind with reasons why you will achieve your goals.

If you are having doubts about your ability to achieve your goals, remember, it's totally natural to have doubts. About 99% of people have doubts about their ability to achieve their goals at some point or another. If you're having doubts, that just shows you're in a process of expansion and in the middle of increasing your ability to manifest. Again, this is normal. You couldn't get where you want to go if you were to stay who you are now.

Part of the reason that we have doubts is because we have picked up on the negativity of others around us. This is also normal and the power these negative thoughts have on you will become less with time. If you feel as though the people in your life are not being sincerely supportive of your goals, limit your exposure to them. It is crucial to keep yourself from being impacted by the beliefs or words of negative people.

A great way to bring your focus back to something positive is to review your list and create another copy of it, putting focus on each item as you write. Do this as often as you like. Also, always know in your heart you are as capable of having as much love, wealth, and happiness as anyone on this planet.

Getting ideas for new goals and desires is a good thing! Generating new wants and goals is part of the process. When this happens, simply take your new goals and add them to the top of your list. If you feel it is better to remove older goals from your list, go right ahead. Again, this is all part of the process and totally normal. Remember, people change and plans change.

If you are like most people, you may have added, "Make more money" to your list. As I've mentioned before, remember to be specific about this and all of your goals. Add to your list exactly how much money you want to make. Set a deadline for when you would like to receive this money. The more specific you are with the details of what you want, the better results will come from your process.

When you are writing your list, add as much detail as possible. For example, if you want a new job, include the specifics of that job. What is your salary? What is your boss like? What does your office look like?

The more details you can add to the description of your goals, the better. Always leave room for "something more" though. It is for this reason that I suggest adding the statement "I want this (or something better)" to the end of every list you create. When timing is concerned, you may want to add, "As quickly as possible."

Writing things down is like placing an order, so think of your list as an order form. How many do you need? What color? What type of "shipping" is needed? The more clear and confident you are in what you want, the faster it will manifest.

Acknowledge your manifestations as they come in. There is no such thing as coincidence and being aware of this will help you to improve your capacity to manifest both quickly and easily.

Remember, the more faith and trust you have in the process, the better it works. Each time you "turn on" the Rich Switch to manifest the results you want and let yourself experience happiness and faith in the process, you will be even better at creating results next time. Your power to use the Rich Switch and the manifestation abilities that come with it will grow in direct proportion to the faith you have in your higher power.

As a reminder, it is very important that you always strive to feel happy and grateful for what you already have in your life. In particular, you want to be grateful to your inner self for manifesting the results you have already received, even before you became aware of this process. The abundance you are looking ahead to already partially exists in your life and your present condition is just as magnificent as the conditions you are seeking.

Combining the instructions above with faith, belief, and gratitude will bring you more than you can consciously imagine.

Infuse Your Words With Even More Power

To help the process above work much faster for you, before you write your list, go through the following steps to help gain clarity and unblock anything that may be keeping you from having what you desire.

Define What You Want

As easy as it sounds, deciding what you want is an important step. It is likely that you are pretty used to thinking about what you can't have or what you don't want. It is time now to start thinking about what you *do* want to achieve in your life.

Change Your Belief Patterns

At first it might be difficult for you to shift your thinking toward what you *do* want. Changing your thoughts can only happen if you change your beliefs about what is truly possible for you to manifest. Holding on to various beliefs becomes habit. As we all know, habits can be hard to break and to turn from negative to positive. However, it can be done. You are capable of doing it.

When you were a baby, someone helped you walk your first steps. Imagine if they taught you to walk in a completely different way than the way you walk now. Instead, they taught you to wave your right hand in the air as you took each step. Now, imagine for a moment, how you would feel if you grew up in a world in which *everyone* waved their right hands in the air when they walked. You would have no idea that any other way of walking was acceptable. You would believe this was the only way to walk properly.

But what if, one day, you had a notion that there was another way? Even though you would question whether it was possible and you might be afraid to go against the norm, you still couldn't let go of the feeling that another way of doing things (or another belief) could become part of your life.

Changing your current beliefs is exactly the same. Some things will be easier to let go of than others. But please keep in mind, those beliefs you know are holding you back from having what you want can be replaced simply by choosing a new belief, fertilizing this new belief with positive thought, and then allowing it to grow into something beautiful.

Recognizing the Power Already Within You

Everyone has a magnificent force inside. This force is powerful and waiting to serve you. This force is known by a variety of different names. It has been called the soul, the unconscious, God, and the Universe. No matter what you call it, it is there for you. Open your heart to this force and let it guide you to your desires.

In order to bring about what you want, you need to do more than just hope for it. The powerful force inside of you needs to be activated. The force is activated by combining belief, faith, and gratitude. Have these three things in the forefront of your mind and you will be unstoppable.

This is important, so I'm going to repeat it in the form of an easy-to-remember equation…

The Rich Switch = Belief + Faith + Gratitude

The more belief, faith, or gratitude you have, the greater your results will be.

If you are having trouble with any of these elements, try to think of current situations in your life where you are easily able to apply them.

For example, if you are having trouble with faith, find something in your life of which you are positive. Do you know the sun will rise tomorrow? Sure you do! Analyze the feeling behind this and transpose it to other aspects in your life. As you see your power to manifest become greater, faith in all aspects of your life will become easier and easier.

Avoid Negativity

It is a good idea to not absorb, or react to, any negativity from your friends, family, co-workers, or any other outside influences you feel are not supportive of you. Instead, focus your energies on what you want to achieve.

The truth is, when we change, everyone who surrounds us changes how they respond to us. The best way for you to avoid negativity is to change the way you respond to it. When someone says something negative, most people either react to it, take it personally, or absorb the negativity within themselves, without saying a word. While you can't stop people from speaking critically, you can begin to consciously respond to their comments and actions rather than react. A good way to do this is to close your eyes and visualize the negative energy bouncing off you and dissipating into the air.

Perhaps you are wondering, "Aren't respond and react the same thing?"

The answer is "no". A "reaction" is automatic, unconscious, and not thought out in advance. When you react, you are doing so based on emotion and ego.

A "response" is a *chosen* action, based on your ability to respond with forethought. When you respond, a certain event happens, and you have a choice as to what will happen next.

How can you best respond to negativity and negative people? When harsh words are spoken toward you, silently make the conscious decision to offer the person who is speaking your compassion and understanding, knowing that hurtful words are only spoken by those who are wounded themselves.

Ideally, it is best to avoid negative people and avoid the situation entirely; however, we are not always ready or able to do this. Once you begin to respond differently toward negativity, such as described above, you will see a shift in negative people as well.

Everyone is on his or her own path and negative people hold an important place in our lives, even if just to show us what type of behavior to avoid. However, do not let the lack of awareness, the fear, and the ignorance of other people hold you back from fulfilling your purpose.

STEP TWO:
You Get What You Give

Giving to charity is an extremely powerful way to activate your Rich Switch. In fact, it's so powerful that there are two ways through which you can both give to charity and help yourself to achieve better results in your life.

The first way to give to charity is through **tithing**.

The traditional definition of tithing was to give 10% of your income to the church. The concept of tithing has come a long way. Today, tithing involves giving part of your income to a charity, person, or concept that you find inspiring

If you are someone who does not tithe because you haven't found an organization that compels you enough to donate, ask yourself how you would like to help others or what you're passionate about?

If you are an entrepreneur, perhaps you want to tithe to an organization like Kiva.org, which allows you to donate money to people in other countries who are creating small businesses. If you are passionate about animals, perhaps you want to tithe to a local animal shelter. You can even tithe directly to an individual who you feel is making a difference in a way you feel is inspiring.

Tithing should *always* involve donating money. Even though you could donate your time to many great causes, for the purpose of this specific exercise, make the choice to give of your money. It is key because this act of donating your money demonstrates to your Higher Power that you believe in a free-flowing system of money. Giving money freely to others will allow money to return easily to you.

Tithing is a way to make the statement that you have abandoned any fears about scarcity or lack of money in your life. You also are confirming that you believe there are enough resources to go around for everyone and that you will always have enough in the way of provisions.

Remember the equation…

The Rich Switch = Belief + Faith + Gratitude

Before you make your donation, make sure you are full of positive energy. When you make the donation, fully enjoy the experience of giving. When you give to charity with no anticipation of getting back anything for yourself, it is a wonderful experience. You are opening your heart, giving of yourself in the most humble way. When you donate to improve the lives of others, and when you give with sincerity and compassion, rewards will always come back to you.

Remember that everything in this book should feel comfortable and have a sense of ease. While tithing is a great way to show your faith in your Higher Power, if you're not there yet, don't let that stop you from donating money at all.

Something which will help you to feel good about giving

money is knowing how much the money you donate will mean to people and how it will improve their lives. A great example of a little money going a long way is a $20 donation to CharityWater.org. This will give a person in Africa clean, safe drinking water for 20 years. I've listed similar charities, where a little money goes a long way, in the back of this book.

Start where you are and build upon it. The important thing is that you do *something*.

If you are not accustomed to donating money to charity, make sure you monitor how you feel before, and after, giving. Chances are you will feel fantastic! After giving money, it is common to feel a surge of positive energy and a general sense of lightness. Knowing you have acted in a way to genuinely help others is a powerful way to use your energy. You will feel a definite sense of joy.

The second part of this charity exercise involves looking through your house and gathering bags of various things you no longer need or use. These things can consist of clothing, furniture, books, souvenirs, shoes, and more. When you look around at your house, if you are like most people, there is some clutter including things you no longer need or use.

When we use the Rich Switch to bring about change in our lives, we are looking to release the energies and attachments from the past.

Anything you no longer need or use is fair game. Even get rid of the things you *might* use someday. Also, if you have objects that you find remind you of your life in the past that you are trying to move away from, these are ideal things to donate to charity. Fill up a big bag (or bags) and give these items to your favorite local charity to benefit other people.

When you want to manifest new and better things into your life, it is a good idea to clear out space to show the Universe you have room for more. Donating old things demonstrates you are anticipating new things to enter your life and you are clearing out space in advance.

Both the tithing exercise, as well as the donation exercise activates the force of positive energy to flow in and out of your life. Gripping on to money or possessions keeps you from having the experience of receiving more than you ever have in the past. Be just as open to releasing as you are to receiving.

Painless Ways to Give to Charity

Many people forego giving to charity because they feel a sense of lack in their own lives. How can you give money away when you need more money?

Although this is counter-intuitive, it is one of the most important aspects of the Rich Switch. Giving money away shows you trust that you will have your needs met.

As has been mentioned previously, everything regarding the Rich Switch should be fun and enjoyable. The secret to getting the most out of this step in the process isn't how much you give, but how you go about giving it.

Here are some suggestions which make charitable giving painless...even for people who think they can't afford to give money away. By following these suggestions, you will see that you have more money that you need and increase your capacity to give painlessly and joyfully in the future.

1. Even $1 Makes a Difference

Dollars add up. Giving $10 a month can make a big difference when it's done by you and several thousand people. Get on an "auto pay" plan and forget about it. Even in the toughest economy, it's unlikely you'll miss $10.

Many grocery stores and fast food restaurants offer the option to "add $1 for charity" when paying. If you're given this option, say "yes"! This money adds up.

2. Got Any Spare Change?

We all do! Save your spare change and donate it at the end of the month.

Coinstar, the self-service coin-counting kiosk, will automatically count your money and donate it to a charity of your choice, including American Red Cross, March of Dimes, World Wildlife Fund, and UNICEF. This program has already raised over $20,000,000.00 for these charities and others.

3. Donate 10% of Your Stuff

Charities like Goodwill and the Salvation Army will

take household items, such as electronics, clothing, books, and furniture, as charitable donations.

Go though items in your home, looking for things you rarely (or never) use. For example, a winter coat you might use a couple of days per year. This takes up space that could be used for something else.

If you "think" you'll use something in the future, give it away. You can always buy another one in the future if needed.

Giving away things is not only a way to help people in need, it also shows you trust your Higher Power to provide for you.

The Bottom Line in Giving to Charity

Whenever you donate money or resources to a cause, you are contributing to something which you feel has importance. Based on the Law of Attraction, whatever energy you put out, must come back to you. In short, taking care of others will make sure you are taken care of as well.

Giving to a cause you believe in shows the Universe not only that you trust you'll be provided for, but also that you understand there is a "higher purpose" for the money in your life. It shows you get the "inter-connectivity" of all living things and that what we call life is about something much bigger than just you.

Whether you decide to donate money or not, it doesn't reflect on how "good" you are as a person. From a Rich Switch perspective, it is far better for you not to donate money, if you feel the donation is forced or makes you resentful.

With that said, if you're not donating money now, I hope you'll stay open to the idea. It's easy to start the habit, with pocket change, and the good results you'll get from doing it are massive.

STEP THREE:
Evoking the Power of the Mastermind

Mastering the Rich Switch is much easier and faster when you have the proper support group in your life. This section of the book is a "bonus" which will help you to find and organize the right people in your life, to combine your power with the power of others, and create a "Super Rich Switch."

Think of how powerful the sun is. It both lights and heats the Earth.

What happens when you put a magnifying glass under the sun's light? That energy is focused in a single spot, which makes it even more powerful.

What if each of your friends grabbed a magnifying glass and joined you in focusing the light they received on the exact same spot?

This section shows you how to focus the power of the Rich Switch in a similar way!

The Mastermind – How to Establish and Run Your Mastermind Group

Are you looking to make great things happen in your life? Do you have an idea of success that you would like to achieve, but feel as though you are not moving quickly enough towards these goals? If these statements sound like they apply to you, a mastermind group could be the perfect solution.

After working with the group, you will find new ideas, solutions, and answers come to you more easily. You will feel more positive and motivated about your life and situations therein.

A mastermind group is ideal if you are working towards goals in your life and feel you need inspiration, empathy, and support. People have found, time and time again, that these groups have powers that will seem almost magical to you as you witness not only your life change, but the lives of others change as well.

Many successful people have used mastermind groups, and most consider their mastermind groups as being vital to their success. While they were in the process of achieving their goals, they met regularly with these groups to discuss their milestones, goals, and how to deal with any particular obstacles they encountered along the way.

Ideally, a mastermind group is usually small in members. The optimal number of members is six or seven. This number is big enough to get varying feedback, yet small enough to where the group can be easily organized.

Because the optimal number of members for a mastermind group is small, it may be difficult to find a group to join. Therefore, if you are looking to be a part of a group, chances are that the best way to do it is to start a new group yourself.

Most people who believe in the principle of the mastermind believe, not just in the achievement of business success, but in personal development success as well. The saying, "like attracts like," not only applies to the people you will attract into your mastermind group, but it is the cornerstone to how each person in the group will go about achieving their success. Simply put, whatever you focus on will result in your receiving more of that in your life.

If you are looking to achieve certain milestones, the best way to achieve them is by focusing on them and what you can put in place to make sure those milestones are inevitable. If you are sitting around your house bemoaning how your goals and milestones are too difficult, the chances are high that you will never obtain these goals.

A successful mastermind group will keep your focus on your goals as well as develop ideas on the conditions you can put in place to make sure those goals happen without question. The feedback and support you'll receive from a mastermind group is invaluable.

When forming your mastermind group, seek out the company of likeminded individuals. You want to surround yourself with driven people who are all working in the same direction as you. Your achievements will be heightened, and most likely will arrive even quicker when you are part of a group of people all focusing on similar things.

Until you have actually experienced participating in a mastermind group yourself, it is easy to discount its importance. The truth of the matter is, participating in a group where all members are helping each other to manifest their goals can be a transformative experience. When you are in a group, you will find yourself surrendering to the process of manifesting and lifted by the power of other people working toward similar goals. There really is no replacement for the positive energy of a group whose members are all seeking to progress in the same direction.

You will find that in a mastermind group, your fellow group members will keep your attitude in check, and offer you support to realign with positive energies when things are not going as expected. You will learn how to improve your own thinking and attitude by hearing stories from your group members.

One of the most important things you will gain from participation in a mastermind group is the impact it has on you at the subconscious level. When you are in a group of like-minded people, you find that you don't have to expend so much energy to motivate yourself. The positive feelings and enthusiasm of the group will lift your spirits and keep you progressing in the right direction.

These days, mastermind groups all over the world are held either by phone or via online chat. While these methods of connecting are convenient and effective, there is no substitution for the dynamic energy which is exchanged when a group meets in person. When you create your group, try to add a local meetup element or, if the group members are located at a distance from where you live, consider planning an event where everyone can get together monthly or at least several times per year.

One of the benefits of joining a mastermind group is that all the members begin to share what is called a **collective mind**. This is much like linking several individual computers together and putting them to work on the same problem.

The premise of a collective mind is to have different minds, with different experiences and specialized knowledge, working together and heading in the same positive direction. In the process of coming together, a "collective conscious" begins to emerge. For this reason, it is important that the people in your mastermind group should share similar modes of thinking and values. Before you begin your group, it is essential to ensure, as best you can, that the members of your mastermind group be "on the same page."

Napoleon Hill first coined the term "mastermind group" in his seminal book **Think and Grow Rich**. Hill described the group as: *"...two or more minds working actively together in perfect harmony towards a common definite object."*

His book, which was written almost 100 years ago, illuminates patterns of how some of the most successful and wealthy people in history approached the achievement of success.

Napoleon Hill wrote how the mastermind group was used by the famous steel magnate and millionaire Andrew Carnegie and how he successfully used mastermind groups in the early days of his career.

Hill wrote:

> *"Mr. Carnegie's mastermind group consisted of a staff of approximately fifty men, with whom he surrounded himself, for the definite power of manufacturing and marketing steel. He attributed his entire fortune to the power he accumulated through this 'Master Mind.' The power of participating in this group was essential in launching Carnegie's career. Many other famous leaders and trailblazers used mastermind groups to achieve rapid and monumental success."*

Starting Your Own Mastermind Group

Now that you understand the importance of a mastermind group, a powerful opportunity awaits you...

Why not begin your own mastermind group? If you decide to begin your own group, you can choose the members, the method of meeting, and the direction of the group. Additionally, if you start your own mastermind group, you'll likely take on the role of the group leader and facilitator. This is a great opportunity for you to grow.

Want to start the group yourself, but have somebody else be the leader? If you pick the right people for your group, there will likely be a suitable person who is eager to be a leader. Perhaps you can alternate leadership with another group member as an option.

Regardless of who leads your group or the specifics as to how it is run, there really should be nothing that holds you back from getting started. There are unlimited possibilities as to how you can run things, so don't get caught up in thinking things must be a certain way. However you decide to do things is the right way.

Establishing a new mastermind group is a great opportunity to be creative and to develop your power to manifest. Like with all areas of your business, and life, you get to create the most ideal experience for you. Yes, there will be some compromising that will need to take place, since you will want to be accommodating to others in the group, but you will be guiding this process.

One of the most important aspects of a mastermind, helping others to achieve their goals, is also one of the most rewarding. This is especially true when you facilitate or lead the group.

When you see other members of your group succeeding and manifesting great things in the world, you will know you had a hand in helping with that success. This is very powerful, as it will be more proof that you are growing in your ability to manifest.

Your ability to manifest is the number one reason for being in a mastermind group. Whether you manifest something for yourself, or help to manifest something for another member, it's all the same. Like any relationship, the one you have with other members in your group will not always be "50/50." Don't worry about this. If you give without "getting back" right away, you are still getting something, which is practice manifesting. Once this skill is adequately developed, you can use it for yourself all you want.

Guidelines for Finding Members for Your Mastermind Group

For better or for worse, people are highly influenced by the other people around them. That's why it is so crucial to avoid spending your time with negative people. Even if you are an extremely strong-minded person, negativity still affects you. We align our feelings and beliefs with those of the people around us.

When you choose your mastermind group members, you can assemble people who you think with work well together and compliment one another in the achievement of their individual hopes and dreams. A great positive energy is gained from the feeling of genuinely helping others to achieve their goals.

There are certain guidelines for finding and choosing members for your mastermind group which will allow the group to be its most beneficial. If you are starting a mastermind group from scratch, follow these guidelines to ensure you have the best experience possible.

1. Find members whom you feel are more successful than you.

When you are looking for members for your mastermind group, it is a good idea to find members whom you feel are more successful than you. However, keep in mind that this rule and the word "successful" does not have to apply just to people who have more money than you. You can have someone in your group that has very little money, but whom you feel is extremely inspiring when it comes to how they handle their personal relationships. Or perhaps you find someone whom, again, has less money than you, but is completely on target with his or her ability to manage time and get things done.

Again, the idea of being successful does not have to apply just to money, so don't just choose members for your group based on who you know is wealthy. After all, as we all know, there are plenty of wealthy people who have negative attitudes and who are struggling in many other areas of life.

The idea here is that you want to choose members for your mastermind group who you can learn from and what you learn will not always be about money. Finding people who have achieved even more than you, in multiple areas, is a great way for you to expand "success" in all areas of your life, not just financial ones.

Ideally, your mastermind group should consist of people who have been successful in many different areas of their lives. Those who get the "big picture" are much more valuable to the group than "specialists" who only get one aspect of success.

Putting together a group with people who have a good life-balance, with success in many things, will set up a great group dynamic which will get you much better results.

2. Find members who are dedicated.

It's important to make sure you find members who are dedicated to the group and its goals. Members need to have the same commitment to attend all meetings, so everyone will receive the maximum benefit. They need to be on time, prepared, and have the ability to focus on each meeting without distraction.

When you connect with a prospective member, you should inquire about this person's vision and future goals, both short and long term, to help you determine if this potential member is truly serious about participating. As it is of paramount importance that this new member will be dedicated to participating in this group, also make sure of his or her ability to complete life tasks and other projects.

Many people say that they are committed and have the best intentions, but simply don't follow through to attend meetings. Others tie up more than their share of group resources, refuse to take responsibility for their own actions, and look at everybody but themselves when something goes wrong. These are not the type of people you want.

When you are meeting potential members, ask questions to get a feel for who they are, but also use your gut instinct to determine whether they are right for the group and ready to manifest. Don't be fooled by slick talkers...they're usually not the ones for whom you are looking.

Once you set a schedule for your mastermind group, be clear that it is everyone's responsibility to attend group meetings on a regular basis. Others who have benefited from mastermind groups in the past have reported that groups function best if the same members are present at each meeting with the same level of commitment and enthusiasm.

If you set a regular schedule and find that there is someone in the group who is missing meetings, shows up late, or leaves early, it may be time for you to politely remove this person from your mastermind group. As mentioned before, many people are simply not ready to put the effort and dedication into their goals like a successful mastermind group requires.

A mastermind group is not for everyone. If you are connected to a person who is not at the same speed as the rest of the group, disharmony occurs. The reason why people miss group meetings is because their subconscious minds guide them not to attend. When you see this happening, let the person go.

In general, don't feel bad turning people down or letting them go. You want to foster a sense of trust among group members. To do this, each member of the group must know other members are equally as dedicated. If you have somebody who isn't dedicated to the group, he or she can poison the entire thing for everyone.

3. Find members who are creative.

When you are choosing members for your mastermind group, seek out individuals whom you feel are following creative and inspiring paths. Make sure you ask people what goals and plans they want to work on in the mastermind group and also what they have to offer the group. When they tell you their ideas, you will likely get a clear insight as to whether or not they're good matches for the group.

You want to find people who are passionate about their goals and excited about their futures. When you find people who seem to have a negative attitude about their goals, it is likely a good idea to pass on asking them to join. Negative people can achieve goals, but negativity does not foster the environment you are looking to cultivate in your mastermind group.

Similarly, you may find people who are excited about their goals, but you don't feel their journeys would be interesting to the rest of the mastermind group. Goals like planting a garden, cleaning clutter, or making an extra $100 per week with a part-time job are all valuable goals and certainly legitimate ones. However, you may feel that people with more dynamic paths ahead of them are a better match. Of course, there are exceptions to this rule.

If you encounter someone and truly feel as though this person would be a great member of the group, even though they do not fit the standard criteria, it is o.k. to accept them. Remember, this is your mastermind group and you can run it any way you like! Even a person with the most basic goals may be the perfect compliment to the other group members. Additionally, this person may grow, develop, and transform through the mastermind group process, becoming a "new" and more dynamic person.

As an example, you may have mastermind members who aspire to run six-figure per year companies and one who aspires to run a non-profit organization. Even though the goals are different, in certain situations, opposites can learn a great deal from each other. Use your best judgment to decide what will work and what won't.

4. Strategies for finding group members.

A strategy many successful mastermind group planners have used is to initially start the group with one or two key people. Most people already know at least one person who would be perfect for a mastermind group. If you have a friend who is determined, motivated and has a positive attitude, he or she may be an ideal candidate.

When you are telling potential members about the group, you can describe to them what your goals are as well as let them know the interests and backgrounds of current members. As you are looking for new members to round out the group, try to match the energy and interests of people already in the group.

Congruency is vital for a successful mastermind group. You don't always have to agree, and you shouldn't always agree, but members must be "on the same page" energetically if you want your group to last.

Don't be afraid to ask people deemed as very successful to join the group holding on to the assumption that someone who has achieved so much would not want to be in a group with people who have not reached their level. Again, you want to learn and grow from people who are very accomplished already.

Keep in mind, just because someone has already been very successful does not mean that they won't feel that your group will bring them even more success. If you pick the right people for your group, regardless of their level of success, everyone will have something to offer.

How to Find a Mastermind Group

If, for whatever reason, you do not want to start your own mastermind group, find a group either in your area or online. To meet in person, you can visit websites like Meetup.com or Craigslist and do a search using the term "mastermind group." You may get lucky and find a group that just happens to be looking for a new member.

If you can't find a mastermind group in your area, consider looking for a Law of Attraction group. Due, in part, to the extremely successful movie **The Secret**, many Law of Attraction groups have been formed around the world. In these groups, people get together to discuss the Law of Attraction principles and to share experiences of deliberate manifestation. Gathering with others who practice the Law of Attraction will be very useful in deepening your belief and strengthening convictions.

If you can find, and choose to join, a Law of Attraction group, you may find members of the group who want to begin a separate mastermind group. Most people who are a part of this sort of group will be working to bring about positive experiences and events in their lives. Start talking with people casually to inquire if they may be interested in starting a smaller group specifically geared to be a mastermind group with focus on a more specific niche, such as business, relationships, or health.

If you are looking to join a mastermind group online, search for message boards where like minded people post messages and interact with each other on a regular basis. Become part of the community and then, once people get to know you, ask people if they would like to start a group separate from the message board.

CONGRATULATIONS!

You've reached the end of the main portion of this book. You now have all the information necessary for taking total command of your Rich Switch and manifesting anything you want.

Should you have a moment of doubt or feel as though you've strayed out of alignment with what you want, re-read this book and re-read your list of goals. Do this as often as you need to.

Give of yourself, your money, and your talents. Show you are grateful. Remember that as you give, you will receive.

Talk to the people in your mastermind group. They are there to help you get back on your path.

You can have all the success you desire and more. You can have everything you want; you just need to believe it will be.

Want a few "secrets" that will make using your Rich Switch easier and the results you get 10x more powerful? Keep reading…

BONUS SECTION 1:

HOW TO MAKE THE RICH SWITCH MORE POWERFUL

Three Techniques to Jumpstart Results When It Feels Like Your Rich Switch Is Not Working

If you have been working to "turn on" your Rich Switch and achieve positive results via the techniques here, and your results are not appearing as you wish, there are various techniques you can use which will free up the flow of positive energy and help you manifest more powerfully.

These techniques will shift you into a more positive frame of mind and allow you to deliberately manifest results that more closely match what you desire. Using these techniques, there is no reason why you won't be able to manifest all of your hopes and dreams in the near future.

If you have you asked yourself, "Why can't I have what I want?", you're not alone. Many people say they are not getting the results they desire. However, keep in mind, the Rich Switch is *always* working…but, like a light switch, it's sometimes in the "off" position.

Whether you are in a positive or negative frame of mind, your Rich Switch is always delivering results to you. Again, like a light switch, just because it's "off" doesn't mean it's broken. You just need to learn how turn it "on" and keep it there.

The nature of the principle behind the Rich Switch, the Law of Attraction, is "**like attracts like**." When you are focusing on the good in your life and moving towards your goals, the Law of Attraction will support you with similar experiences. When you are feeling negative and off track, the Law of Attraction will provide you with experiences you do not necessarily want, but are drawing to yourself because of what you think, feel, and believe.

People who are new to working with the Law of Attraction often try to manifest positive experiences, but find they aren't getting the results they intended. Like any new skill, working with the Law of Attraction is something which improves over time.

The following four essential techniques will set the Law of Attraction into motion for you in a positive way and activate your Rich Switch.

When you are reading about these activities, remember that manifesting your goals through the Law of Attraction should be fun. If you are working toward your goals and you find it feels like work instead of fun, you may be progressing in the wrong direction.

Your thoughts and actions should feel inspired. When you are "in the zone" of acting and feeling confident, and pleased with the actions you are taking, that is the time in which you are manifesting in the most optimal way.

The following techniques are offered in the spirit of enjoyment and will help you to use your Rich Switch more effectively. I've also included several "bonus" techniques, related to forming a group of like-minded individuals, which will be a compliment to all the other processes you currently use when manifesting and give you additional support.

Even if you are already thinking about positive results most of the time, and manifesting in a positive state of feeling, these techniques will still be beneficial to you as they will allow your emotions to be freed up from any negativity in your past to better match your positive thoughts in the present. When working with these techniques, if you find any of them aren't fun or are stressing you out in any way, feel free to move on to the next one.

This is the time for you to boost your manifesting skills and turn on your Rich Switch!

Negativity-Free Day

A very transformative exercise you can practice to activate your Rich Switch is to go an entire day without saying anything negative to anyone.

On your negativity-free day, you should avoid stating anything negative about:

- Circumstances in your life

- Other people
- Observations you make about the world around you
- Yourself

When you wake up in the morning, pay attention to your first thoughts and the words you speak. Your first, early-morning thoughts set the tone for the entire day. If you observe your thoughts becoming dark and cloudy, quickly change them to something positive, before any negative words have a chance to come out of your mouth.

Go about your day as though it were any other day, but make sure everything you say is positive, or at the very least, neutral. At first, you may feel as though this task is somewhat of an impossible feat. In fact, many people slip on their first try. It's o.k. If you do, just get back on track and commit to being more mindful of what it is you are thinking and saying.

With practice, you will find yourself having a gentle control over your mind and what you choose to think. Instead of reacting without thought, you will respond consciously.

If you wake up on your negativity-free day and are feeling terrible, acknowledge this, but do not allow it to control you. You are in control and have the power to respond consciously rather than react automatically and without thought.

Rather than letting negative feelings overcome you and set the tone for every conversation you have and your overall mood, decide what you need to do in order to make yourself feel (even just a bit) better. Take care of yourself and focus on this aspect of your day rather than staying stuck in a negative thought pattern.

Whenever you speak negative words, take a moment to decide if they serve a positive purpose. Most often they do not. Even though you may want to express your displeasure over something or communicate to someone just how much emotional pain you are in, there is still a more peaceful and graceful way of getting your point across without using harsh, negative words.

Understand that, when it comes to the Law of Attraction, the energy and intention that you are constantly putting out impacts how well you manifest your desires and the power of your Rich Switch. If, for example, your goal is to manifest money, when you get frustrated and speak harshly to a co-worker, a spouse or a child, even though that situation seemingly has nothing to do with the money you want to manifest, in truth, your negativity is keeping the money away from you.

When you express negativity, not only do you bring your energy down, you also bring down the energy of those around you. Even if you are speaking funny, negative insults about others, and getting laughs from friends or co-workers, your jokes are really, in actuality, potentially hurtful to everyone—including you. This, of course, is directly related to your own happiness.

If, at first, you can't commit to being negativity-free for an entire day, just commit to an hour. Can't do that? Try for 15 minutes. Still too long? Try five minutes. If that doesn't work, simply focus on the present moment. All we really have is our present moment, so build upon this and you'll soon be negativity-free all the time!

Remember, everything in this book should be fun and enjoyable! A great way to practice being negativity-free, as well as a great way to build a support system of positive people in your life, is to find a friend and make the promise to each other to have a negativity-free conversation.

Notice while you are speaking when your thoughts potentially start to switch to something negative. If and when you sense this happening, switch your focus to something new. If you can't think of anything positive to say, focus on the birds, the trees--anything other than negative thoughts. Your brain can only think about one thing at a time, so put something positive in it, rather than thinking about "not" doing something "negative".

When you pay attention to your thought process and become more aware of your habits of thinking, your Rich Switch will become more powerful. In order to change your habits though, you first need to be aware of them.

Always remember, what you attract in your life is based on your thoughts, feelings, and actions. The Rich Switch is activated by positivity. If you are following all of the manifestation steps to the letter, but are focused on negativity most of the time, you are counteracting the receipt of positive results. The best and quickest manifestations will arrive when your thoughts and feelings are positive and clear, and you are making dedicated steps toward achieving your goals.

Practiced on a regular basis, the negativity-free day will change your life.

The "Thank You" Letter

Another technique you might want to try is called the **Thank You** letter. This is an exercise in which, through the process of writing, you bring your dreams and desires into reality.

Remember the equation I gave you earlier...

The Rich Switch = Belief + Faith + Gratitude

This letter-writing exercise is extremely effective because it helps to develop your belief, faith, and gratitude. Like the list you made initially, this exercise is also extremely powerful since it is a physical manifestation of your thoughts and feelings.

The exercise is simple... Write down all of your desires as though they have already happened and are part of your present reality.

Get a nice notebook, a pen with which you are comfortable writing, and sit down in a quiet and safe place where you won't be interrupted. Next, take a few deep breaths to relax. At the top of the page, write "Dear Universe," "Dear Spirit," "Dear God," "Dear Rich Switch," or whatever salutation makes you feel most comfortable. This letter is going to be written to the higher power you believe is helping to bring all that you desire into your life.

Now, think about what it is you would like to manifest and begin writing a "thank you letter" about it as though you have already received it. Start your letter with, "I am writing to say thank you for..." and list the things that you want to attain in your life as if they are already there.

Let yourself start writing freely about exactly what you've received, how it felt to get it, and how it has changed your life. Express how grateful you are for finally having this desire become part of your life. Get in the feeling of already having it. Recount to your higher power how amazed you were at how easily it came to you, how surprised you were by how easily everything unfolded, and how much joy you felt once it did.

While writing, it is important not to censor yourself. Just let your subconscious freely put your words down on paper.

Stay relaxed and open to inspiration. Allow yourself to believe anything is possible and allow yourself to visualize your ideas in detail. Feel free to write as much intricate detail and description as you can. Remember, it is important to describe everything in the present tense. You want to get the immediate benefit of all the enthusiasm, excitement, and gratitude that comes from experiencing your desires even before they happen. Experiencing the power of all of these emotions before your desire appears in your life will help it come to you faster. Oftentimes, the feeling of elation is actually better than the manifestation itself.

While you are writing your thank you letter, as well as after you have completed it, you should feel warm, positive energy buzzing through your whole body. These positive energies are an indication that you are in the process of manifesting your desires.

Don't let yourself get distracted by worrying about how your desires will manifest or what strategies you need to take in order to make them happen. You should just relax, trust, and stay in a constant state of gratitude. Of course, if you happen to have an inspiration while writing about what you want to manifest and what conditions you can put in place to make sure it happens, feel free to embrace and explore the idea! However, don't struggle or force solutions. You want the answers to flow to and through you.

Emotional Freedom Technique

Emotional Freedom Technique (or **EFT**) is a very useful tool you can use to jumpstart your Rich Switch. EFT is actually a form of acupuncture that you can administer on yourself to access the energy channels that run through your body.

Emotional Freedom Technique can be used effectively with a variety of addictions, and illnesses. EFT founder Gary Craig writes, "EFT often works where nothing else will."

Essentially, EFT clears blocked energy and releases these blocks that may be having a negative impact on our physical and mental health.

Not only does EFT work on illnesses, but it also helps to release emotional blocks that potentially keep your Rich Switch from being "on" and working to your benefit. If you have been trying to manifest positive results and aren't seeing what you want, you may have an emotional block that is holding you back. Through use of Emotional

Freedom Technique, you can clear this block and get on with manifesting your dreams at a much faster pace.

Many people who are trying to manifest results via the Rich Switch find that once they release their emotional blocks with EFT, the process of deliberate manifestation becomes effortless. When you are using the process outlined in this book, it isn't just about what you think, but also what your emotions are resonating. Therefore, even if you are *thinking* positive thoughts, if your emotions aren't on target with your thoughts, your manifestations will be mixed. By bringing in a physical activity, such as EFT, to your manifesting, you will find that *feeling* positive becomes easier for you. Positive feeling is what keeps your Rich Switch activated and working to your advantage.

When you practice EFT, you stimulate meridian points throughout the body through a series of tapping motions with your fingertips on designated points throughout the body. The concept is based on Chinese medicine techniques than have been practiced for thousands of years. Some people have experienced dramatic change in the way they feel after doing even just one session of EFT.

EFT is easy to learn and can be used anywhere and as much as you like.

Rather than giving specific instruction on how to practice EFT, I encourage you, instead, to seek out one of the many of instructional videos you can find online so you can watch how it is done. Learning how to use EFT is much easier by viewing than by reading about it. Having said that, once you have seen EFT in action (and have tried it on yourself), you may want to check out an entire book I've written on the subject of EFT and how to use it to create more money in your life. It's called "10-Day Money Makeover – Simple Steps to Create More Money and Financial Prosperity Using Emotional Freedom Technique (EFT)" and is available wherever books are sold, including Amazon.com.

The Law of Attraction, your Rich Switch, and the Emotional Freedom Technique really do all work hand in hand.

If you are struggling in any way to manifest positive results using the Rich Switch, what will help you to ease this struggle is to simply feel better.

When unresolved issues from your past hinder you, it isn't always easy to raise your vibration on your own. Reliving a painful past through your memories and fears holds you back from manifesting a better life. Sometimes, holding on to your past experiences results in negative energy that literally gets stuck in your body. All of the techniques above are meant to help dissolve those negative blocks.

Once you clear your energy blocks, you will feel as though you have a new lease on life. When restrictions have been released, you will be freed up to effortlessly manifest your hopes and dreams.

BONUS SECTION 2:
MASTERMIND OUTLINES

How to Run Your Mastermind Group Meetings

The best way to start your group is to dive right in and start organizing. It is a good rule of thumb to follow your positive energy and inspiration when you have it. When you have the spark of enthusiasm to start your mastermind group, that time is very likely the right time to begin.

Here are some good general guidelines to follow in order to get the most out of your meeting experiences.

1. A good rule of thumb is to have about 6-7 people in your group and schedule a weekly meeting.

Whether you are conducting the meeting over the phone or in person, schedule your meetings to happen weekly—at the same time and on the same day. You may find scheduling a day and time to accommodate everyone a bit difficult. The truth is, if your group is serious about wanting to experience the benefits of being part of a mastermind, they will be flexible and find a way to be available at the appointed time.

2. Decide on the length of your meetings.

Having a set time and place will encourage the members to focus and work towards the most value within the limits of the meeting time. Mastermind meetings typically should be 60-90 minutes. This gives you enough time to get things done, but not so much time that you get off task.

3. Find a location and/or mode of communication for the mastermind group which works for all members.

If you are meeting in person, use a location that you like and somewhere you feel comfortable. Your group can meet in a coffee shop, a member's living room, or a restaurant. Your group can also meet outside in the park during nice weather. As long as you feel comfortable sharing and giving information, and can stay focused, anywhere is fine.

If you are holding your meetings via phone, you can choose to use a teleconference line (there are several free options available…check online to find them) or use a computer software, which will let you connect via the Internet.

4. At each meeting, choose one person to be the focus.

During each meeting, have a "hot seat" in which one person's goals and obstacles are discussed. The meeting can explore this person's particular challenges and progress on a specific project or goal. Encourage the other people in the group to offer suggestions and brainstorm as to how to help this person. Remember, when your group members help one another, everyone involved will be learning, developing, and benefiting from the process.

5. Choose an "outline" for your meetings.

Having an outline for your mastermind meetings will help things to run smoothly, make sure everyone stays on task, and allow members to walk away with the feeling of having accomplished something, rather than that of having wasted an hour (or more) in idle chatter.

Remember, this is not a social group, although there are certainly social elements. A mastermind group has a specific and definitive purpose, which should be the focus when coming up with an outline for group meetings.

A basic format for a mastermind meeting is to have one member and his or her current situation as the focus. Allow this person to talk within the scheduled time for as much as is needed. After he or she is done speaking, the other mastermind group members can take turns offering their feedback and suggestions. This is, by far, the most powerful part of people coming together to share their goals and struggles. With the remaining meeting time, allow all the members to give a brief update on how they are doing.

This is a basic format. As previously mentioned, you are in charge and can design a format that works best for you and your mastermind group. Two proven and successful "meeting outlines" are included below, to give you something to start with and from which to work. They can be taken as-is or edited in any way.

Another idea is to encourage your members to have an item they find significant to share with the others. This can be an inspiring song, web site, video, or book. As meeting outlines can change over time, depending on the current needs of the group, this particular suggestion might be one you implement after the group has been going for some time.

Feel free to come up with creative ideas for meetings to keep everything fresh for your members. You want them to feel inspired at meetings. As the group leader, use your imagination to bring new elements to the group.

Since, each week, group members are helping each other with suggestions and inspirations, it is crucial to choose people for the group whom you feel are intelligent and motivated. It's also important to get into a mode in which there is a comfortable level of conversation between members. You want each member to feel at ease while offering feedback and suggestions to others in the group.

A solid format for each meeting will enable you to experience one of the exciting aspects of a mastermind group. When group members know their "hot seat" meetings are coming up and the format which the meeting will have, they'll be extra motivated and engaged in the process of giving encouragement and advice to others in the group. They'll be able to focus properly on helping the other members, knowing that they will receive the same opportunities within the coming weeks.

Within your group, it is important to establish some guidelines that apply to each meeting. Make sure members give each other ample time to speak and explore each other's unique issues and goals. It is important that everyone in the group shares the spotlight equally. It is important for members not to just give one another advice, but to act as partners in the goal of manifesting.

Sample Mastermind Group Meeting Outlines

Here are a couple of "outlines" for you to use in your mastermind group. You can use a combination of the two or make your own, if neither of the formats here work for you. You are in charge!

Sample Meeting Outline 1:

Welcome/Agenda – Leader welcomes everybody and goes over agenda for the meeting. The total time for this section of the meeting should take about five minutes.

Teaching – A selected member of the group teaches other members about something related to the focus of the group. For example, if the focus of your group is marketing your business and getting more customers, the member in charge of this section could teach other members about a concept or technique which helped him or her make this happen. A "book report" is great for this section. Total time on this section is about 10 minutes.

Hot Seat – Member on the "hot seat" answers the following questions:

    1. What is your biggest challenge?
    2. What is your biggest opportunity?

This section of the meeting, assuming the total meeting is 60 minutes, should take about 30 minutes. The member answering these questions should talk in detail about what he or she is working on and needs help to accomplish. During this time, other members will ask questions and give advice so the "hot seat" member can move forward more easily.

Commitments – In the last section of the meeting, usually about 15 minutes, group members make a commitment to accomplish a specific task, leading to a specific goal, by the next meeting. This section is also the time to "check in" about previous commitments and let other group members know if you are on task.

Sample Meeting Outline 2:

Welcome/Agenda – Leader welcomes everybody and goes over agenda for the meeting. The total time for this section of the meeting should take about five minutes.

Hot Seat – Member on the "hot seat" answers the following questions:
1. What are you working on?
2. What's working for you?
3. With what do you need help?

This section of the meeting, assuming the total meeting is 60 minutes, should take about 30 minutes. The member answering these questions should talk in detail about what he or she is working on and needs help accomplishing. During this time, other members will ask questions and give advice so the "hot seat" member can move forward more easily.

The 4th Question – In the last section of the meeting, usually about 15 minutes, group members will answer this question…

*"Who can help (hot seat member) with
(hot seat member's problem)?"*

This is the time for group members to take ownership for the solution to the problem with which the "hot seat" member is dealing. For example, if the problem is something such as a legal issue and another group member has a personal connection with a good attorney, that group member could say, "I've got a great attorney I work with and I'll be happy to give him a call for you and make the introduction."

APPENDIX:
Charity Suggestions

As giving money away is one of the best ways to positively activate the Law of Attraction, the following is a list of charities where donating what most people reading this book will consider a small amount of money, will dramatically improve the lives of those who receive the donations.

Donating money to the charities listed below, or charities like them, is especially powerful, since many donation recipients are children, and none will be able to repay you.

Charity Water – charitywater.org

$20 can give a person in Africa clean, safe drinking water for 20 years.

Smile Train – smiletrain.org

$250 provides life-changing cleft lip and palate surgery to children in developing countries.

International Children's Heart Foundation – babyheart.org

One child can have life-saving heart surgery for $2000.

More options...

Visit idealist.org and guidestar.org for more charity options, including searchable databases of non-profit organizations and other information to help you make informed giving decisions.

Final Thoughts on the Rich Switch...

To the Reader of the Rich Switch –

Things we take for granted on a daily basis are truly gifts from the Universe. The majority of people go about each day taking the human body, Earth, and the world around us for granted. However, when we take a moment to think about it, we realize these items truly are miraculous.

In the same way, we often take the beauty and importance of ideas for granted. This book, for example, has powerful ideas that can be easily dismissed.

I believe it is vitally important in life to try to make the lives of other people better. When you have an idea and feel strongly it can benefit another person, you should pass it along. That's the reason I've put together this book and priced it so low.

Every time we give without expecting anything in return, we receive abundance. The Law of Reciprocity works.

If you have been touched by this book, I encourage you to help circulate it and its ideas. Request that it be added to your local library, tell a friend about it, and give away copies to those who can use this information.

To help you do this, I'm offering this book "at cost" to those needing 10 or more copies. Visit RichSwitch.com for complete details and order information.

You will be rewarded beyond your wildest dreams when you give with no expectation of what you will get in return! Go ahead and give, you will be amazed at the results.

BoldThoughts.com presents:

10-Day Money
Makeover

**Simple Steps to Create More Money & Financial Prosperity
Using Emotional Freedom Technique (EFT)**

David Hooper

DAVID HOOPER

ASK, BELIEVE, RECEIVE

7 Days to Increased Wealth,
Better Relationships, and a Life You Love
(...Even When it Seems Impossible)

CPSIA information can be obtained at www.ICGtesting.com
Printed in the USA
244075LV00001B/28/P